D1205512

✳ Smithsonian

LITTLE EXPLORER

AMPHIBIANS

A 4D BOOK

by Sally Lee

PEBBLE
a capstone imprint

Download the Capstone 4D app!

- Ask an adult to download the Capstone 4D app.
- Scan the cover and stars inside the book for additional content.

When you scan a spread, you'll find fun extra stuff to go with this book! You can also find these things on the web at www.capstone4D.com using the password: amphibians.26424

Smithsonian Little Explorer is published by Pebble, 1710 Roe Crest Drive, North Mankato, Minnesota 56003 www.mycapstone.com

Copyright © 2019 by Pebble, a Capstone imprint. All rights reserved. No part of this publication may be reproduced in whole or in part, or stored in a retrieval system, or transmitted in any form or by any means, electronic, mechanical, photocopying, recording, or otherwise, without written permission of the publisher.

The name of the Smithsonian Institution and the sunburst logo are registered trademarks of the Smithsonian Institution. For more information, please visit www.si.edu.

Library of Congress Cataloging-in-Publication Data
Names: Lee, Sally, 1943– author.
Title: Amphibians : a 4D book / by Sally Lee.
Description: North Mankato, Minnesota : an imprint of Pebble, [2019] | Series: Smithsonian little explorer. Little zoologist | Audience: Age 4–8. | Includes bibliographical references and index. Identifiers: LCCN 2018004115 (print) | LCCN 2018008478 (ebook) | ISBN 9781543526547 (eBook PDF) | ISBN 9781543526424 (hardcover) | ISBN 9781543526486 (paperback)
Subjects: LCSH: Amphibians—Juvenile literature.
Classification: LCC QL644.2 (ebook) | LCC QL644.2 .L45 2019 (print) | DDC 597.8—dc23
LC record available at https://lccn.loc.gov/2018004115

Editorial Credits
Michelle Hasselius, editor; Kazuko Collins, designer; Svetlana Zhurkin, media researcher; Kris Wilfahrt, production specialist

Our very special thanks to XX, for her review. Capstone would also like to thank Kealy Gordon, Product Development Manager, and the following at Smithsonian Enterprises: Ellen Nanney, Licensing Manager; Brigid Ferraro, Vice President, Education and Consumer Products; and Carol LeBlanc, Senior Vice President, Education and Consumer Products.

Image Credits
Alamy: Henk Wallays, 14–15; Dreamstime: Kcmatt, 20; Getty Images: Joseph T Collins, 12 (left), The Washington Post/Matt McClain, 24; iStockphoto: Hailshadow, 6; Minden Pictures: Michael and Patricia Fogden, 23 (top); Newscom: Danita Delimont Photography/David R. Frazier, 5; Science Source: Dante Fenolio, 8, 9; Shutterstock: A Cotton Photo, 17 (right), Aliaksei Hintau, 17 (left), davemhuntphotography, 29, Dirk Ercken, 21, Eric Isselee, 28, Ezume Images, 13, Ivan Kuzmin, cover, Jay Ondreicka, 18–19, K Hanley CHDPhoto, 1, Klaus Ulrich Mueller, 26, Michael Lynch, 25, Michiel de Wit, 2–3, 12 (right), Milan Zygmunt, 7, reptiles4all, 11, Robert Lessmann, 27, Steve Byland, 16, tristan tan, 19 (inset); SuperStock: NaturePL, 23 (bottom)

Printed and bound in the United States.
PA021

TABLE OF CONTENTS

SMITHSONIAN'S NATIONAL ZOO

In 1887 Smithsonian scientist William Temple Hornaday traveled to the western United States. He expected to see millions of American bison. But hunters had nearly killed off the species. Hornaday wanted to help the American bison and other endangered animals. He brought 15 animal species back with him to the Smithsonian Institution in Washington, D.C. Over the years, more animals were brought to the Zoo. Today there about 1,800 animals at the Smithsonian's National Zoo.

In 1974 the Smithsonian's National Zoo created the Smithsonian Conservation Biology Institute (SCBI). Here, scientists work to help save endangered species from all over the world.

The Reptile Discovery Center is home to more than 70 reptile and amphibian species.

ZOO WORKERS

keeper: provides daily care to the animals, including training, feeding, and cleaning their Zoo habitats

veterinarian: responsible for the health of the animals; vets treat sick animals and keep others healthy

volunteer: unpaid person who may help with zoo tours, small animal care, answering questions, and helping with special events

wildlife educator: organizes fact sheets about wildlife, summer camps, and special events to teach visitors about various animals

zoo scientist: provides scientific help to care for animals and researches ways to save endangered species

Two areas of the Smithsonian's National Zoo have amphibians—the Reptile Discovery Center and Amazonia. In both places, amphibians live in settings similar to their natural habitats. Many of the amphibians are endangered. Visitors learn what scientists are doing to help them.

AFRICAN CLAWED FROG

African clawed frogs have smooth bodies, which are covered with mucus. The mucus protects their skin. African clawed frogs live in pools of standing water. They come to the surface to breathe.

These frogs are 2 to 4 inches (5 to 10 centimeters) long. They live in eastern and southern Africa. African clawed frogs eat insects, shrimp, small fish, tadpoles, and anything else they can grab. The frogs don't have tongues. They use their fingers to shove food into their mouths.

The African clawed frog's eyes and nostrils are on top of its head. This way it can see and breathe without being seen by predators.

An African clawed frog swims underwater.

Male African clawed frogs don't have vocal cords. But they can make a clicking sound by tightening their throat muscles.

Aquatic caecilians look like giant earthworms. But they are actually legless amphibians. Aquatic caecilians can grow to 22 inches (56 cm) long. They live in lowland rivers and streams in Columbia and Venezuela.

Caecilians are blind. They have tiny tentacles on their upper jaws that sense their preys' movements.

Aquatic caecilians are also called rubber eels.

In the wild, aquatic caecilians live between 4 and 5 years. The ones at the Smithsonian's National Zoo are more than 10 years old.

Aquatic caecilians feed on insect larvae, worms, and small fish. They grab their prey with their peglike teeth. At the Zoo they are fed earthworms, raw shrimp strips, and squid tentacles.

CORONATED TREE FROG

Coronated tree frogs are 3 inches (7.6 cm) tall. They live in warm mountain forests in Central America.

Coronated tree frogs rest during the day and hunt for insects at night. The frogs make loud calls that can be heard 300 feet (91 meters) away. At the Zoo coronated tree frogs are fed crickets, mealworms, and earthworms.

The female coronated tree frog lays between 50 and 300 eggs. Less than 25 of these eggs will hatch.

Coronated tree frogs are also called spiny-headed tree frogs. This is because they have pointed bumps on their heads.

EASTERN RED-BACKED SALAMANDER

Eastern red-backed salamanders are found in the eastern United States and Canada. They are 2 to 5 inches (5 to 12.7 cm) long. These salamanders don't have lungs. They breathe through their skin, which absorbs oxygen. They cannot breathe if their skin dries out. These salamanders live in damp areas under logs or near streams to keep their skin moist.

Salamanders can detach their tails when threatened. The tails grow back later.

Some red-backed salamanders have red stripes down their backs. Others have gray backs.

JEWELS OF APPALACHIA

Appalachia's streams and forests are ideal habitats for salamanders. This area is home to more salamander species than any other place in the world. The Jewels of Appalachia exhibit at the Smithsonian's National Zoo gives visitors a look at the underground world of salamanders from this area.

Eastern red-backed salamanders eat worms and insects. At the Zoo, keepers feed them crickets, fruit flies, bean beetles, and black worms.

EMPEROR NEWT

Emperor newts live in the Yunnan province in China. They grow to 6 inches (15 cm) long. These newts are dark brown. They have yellow or orange coloring on their heads, backs, tails, and front and back legs.

The female emperor newt lays up to 100 eggs at a time.

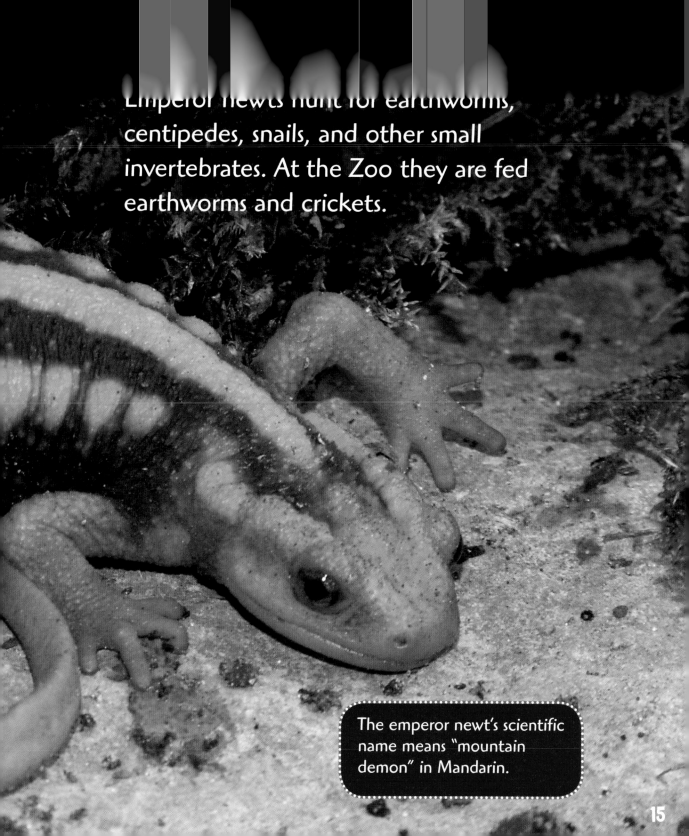

Emperor newts hunt for earthworms, centipedes, snails, and other small invertebrates. At the Zoo they are fed earthworms and crickets.

The emperor newt's scientific name means "mountain demon" in Mandarin.

FOWLER'S TOAD

Fowler's toads are poisonous toads that live in the northeastern United States and southeastern Canada. Most live in woodlands, river valleys, ponds, marshlands, and fields. These small toads are less than 3.5 inches (9 cm) long. They hunt at night for insects, snails, and worms. At the Zoo they are fed crickets and earthworms.

FROG OR TOAD?

frogs	toads
smooth, moist skin	dry, bumpy skin
high, bulging eyes	lower, football-shaped eyes
long hind legs, making them good jumpers	short hind legs, so they run or take small hops

The female Fowler's toad lays eggs in strings that contain up to 20,000 eggs.

HELLBENDER

Hellbenders are the largest salamanders in North and South America. They can be 29 inches (74 cm) in length. They weigh up to 5 pounds (2.3 kilograms). Hellbenders live under rocks in fast-flowing rivers. The large salamanders dart out of the rocks to eat crayfish, worms, or small fish that swim by.

At the Zoo, hellbenders are fed crayfish, shrimp, smelt, and earthworms.

Chinese giant salamander

Hellbenders are not the largest salamanders in the world. Chinese giant salamanders can be 6 feet (1.8 meters) long.

Hellbenders are covered with slippery mucus. This is why they are nicknamed snot otters.

LEMUR TREE FROG

Lemur tree frogs may be extinct one day. These tiny frogs once filled the mountain forests and moist lowlands of Central America. Now they are only found in small areas of Costa Rica, Columbia, and Panama. These frogs are 1 to 2 inches (2.5 to 5 cm) long and can change colors. During the day, they are lime green to match the leaves they rest on. At night their bodies turn brown to blend in with their surroundings.

Lemur tree frogs hunt for insects and small invertebrates. At the Zoo the frogs are fed crickets, fruit flies, and worms.

Lemur tree frogs do not have webbed fingers or toes like other frogs.

Scientists believe the lemur tree frog's skin allows it to stay in the sun longer without drying out.

HELPING THE ENDANGERED

Nearly 30 percent of amphibians are in danger of becoming extinct. Smithsonian scientists have joined with other groups to help save these animals. They collect healthy amphibians and breed them in labs and zoos to increase their populations. Then scientists safely return the amphibians to the wild.

ORIENTAL FIRE-BELLIED TOAD

Oriental fire-bellied toads look like ordinary green toads. But if you look underneath, their stomachs are bright orange or red. These toads are 2 inches (5 cm) long. They spend most of their time in slow-moving streams and ponds in parts of China and Russia. They hibernate in the winter inside rotting logs or leaf piles.

In the wild these toads eat worms, mollusks, and insects. At the Zoo, keepers feed them small crickets three times a week.

When threatened, Oriental fire-bellied toads ooze a milky substance from their skin. This can hurt a predator's mouth and eyes.

THE UNKEN REFLEX

Oriental fire-bellied toads use their bodies to warn predators that they're toxic. The toads get into a position called the Unken reflex. They rise up and arch their backs to show the bright red coloring underneath. Amphibians with bright coloring are often poisonous.

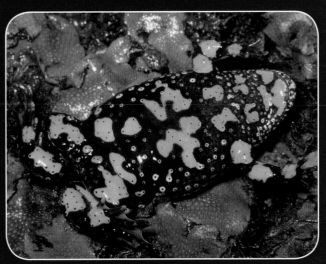

PANAMANIAN GOLDEN FROG

Panamanian golden frogs were once commonly found in the mountain rain forests in Panama. Then the deadly chytrid fungus spread through the golden frog population. Now the frogs are extinct in the wild.

Smithsonian scientists are part of the Panama Amphibian Rescue and Conservation Project. This group is working to keep Panama's amphibian species from going extinct.

THE KILLER FUNGUS

The world's frog population is decreasing. One cause is the deadly chytrid fungus. The fungus damages the frog's skin, making it hard for them to breathe and take in water. The frogs die when their skin becomes too damaged.

The Panamanian golden frogs make a powerful toxin that protects them from predators. Scientists believe this toxin is made from the insects they eat. At the Zoo the Panamanian golden frogs are not fed these insects, so they are not toxic. Keepers feed the frogs bean beetles, fruit flies, and crickets.

POISON FROGS

Poison frogs are tiny, colorful, and toxic. They live in wet tropical forests in Central and South America. The poison frogs use their long, sticky tongues to catch ants, termites, and other small insects.

Poison frogs are only about 0.75 to 1.5 inches (1.9 to 3.8 cm) long.

The Zoo has three species of poison frogs—the green and black poison frog, the tri-colored poison frog, and the blue poison frog. They are fed small crickets, bean beetles, worms, and fruit flies. The frogs are not toxic on this diet.

Poison frogs are also called poison arrow frogs and poison dart frogs. Some American Indian tribes poisoned their arrows by rubbing them on the frogs' skin.

VIETNAMESE MOSSY FROG

Vietnamese mossy frogs are hard to see. They look like clumps of green moss. The frogs live in the rocky cliffs and rain forests of northern Vietnam. They are good climbers thanks to the sticky pads at the end of their toes.

Vietnamese mossy frogs are about 3.5 inches (8 cm) long. Males are usually smaller and thinner than females. At night the frogs hunt for crickets, cockroaches, and other large insects. At the Zoo they are fed insects and earthworms.

Vietnamese mossy frogs can fold into a ball and play dead when frightened.

Vietnamese mossy frogs can make their voices sound as if they are 10 to 13 feet (3 to 4 m) away.

GLOSSARY

bulging—sticking out in a rounded lump

endangered—at risk of dying out

extinct—no longer living; an extinct animal is one that has died out, with no more of its kind

fungus—a living thing similar to a plant, but without flowers, leaves, or green coloring; mold is a type of fungus

habitat—the natural place and conditions where a plant or animal lives

hibernate—to spend winter in a deep sleep

invertebrate—an animal that has no backbone

larva—an insect at the stage of development between an egg and an adult

lowland—an area of land that is lower than the surrounding country

Mandarin—China's official language

mollusk—a soft-bodied creature that usually has a shell

mucus—a slimy, thick fluid

nostril—one of the two outside openings in the nose used to breathe and smell

oxygen—a colorless gas that people and animals breathe

predator—an animal that hunts other animals for food

prey—an animal hunted by another animal for food

species—a group of plants or animals that have the same ancestor and common characteristics

tentacle—a long, armlike body part some animals use to touch, grab, or smell

toxic—poisonous

webbed—folding skin or tissue between an animal's toes or fingers

CRITICAL THINKING QUESTIONS

1. Describe a keeper's role at the Smithsonian's National Zoo.

2. Oriental fire-bellied toads hibernate during the winter. Why do you think these toads hibernate? How does this help them?

3. How do Vietnamese mossy frogs protect themselves from predators?

READ MORE

Berne, Emma Carlson. *Amphibians.* My First Animal Kingdom Encyclopedias. North Mankato, Minn.: Capstone Press, 2017.

Gillespie, Katie. *Poison Dart Frog.* Eyediscover. New York: AV2 by Weigl, 2016.

Hall, Katharine. *Amphibians and Reptiles: A Compare and Contrast Book.* Compare and Contrast Book. Mt. Pleasant, S.C.: Arbordale Publishing, 2015.

INTERNET SITES

Use FactHound to find Internet sites related to this book.

Visit www.facthound.com

Just type in 9781543526424 and go.

Super-cool stuff!

Check out projects, games and lots more at
www.capstonekids.com

INDEX